#Help!
Study Hacks

How Do I
Write Well?

Sarah Eason and Louise Spilsbury

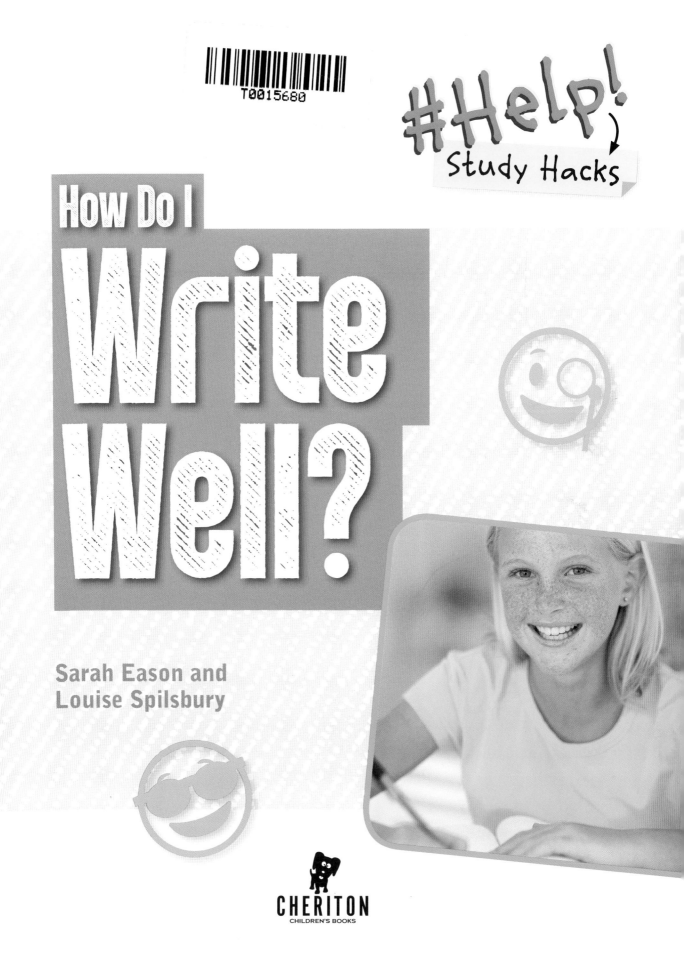

CHERITON
CHILDREN'S BOOKS

Please visit our website, www.cheritonchildrensbooks.com to see more of our high-quality books.

First Edition

Published in 2022 by **Cheriton Children's Books**
PO Box 7258, Bridgnorth WV16 9ET, UK

© 2022 Cheriton Children's Books

Authors: Sarah Eason and Louise Spilsbury
Designer: Paul Myerscough
Editor: Jennifer Sanderson
Picture Researcher: Rachel Blount
Proofreader: Wendy Scavuzzo

Picture credits: Cover: Shutterstock/sunabesyou. Inside: p1: Shutterstock/michaeljung; p4: Shutterstock/Asier Romero; p5: Shutterstock/santypan; p6: Shutterstock/Ben Gingell; p7: Shutterstock/AnnaStills; p8: Shutterstock/bogumil; p9: Shutterstock/Gecko1968; p10: Shutterstock/Africa Studio; p11: Shutterstock/Susan Schmitz; p12: Shutterstock/Monkey Business Images; p13: Shutterstock/slowmotiongli; p14: Shutterstock/Len44ik; p15: Shutterstock/Namart Pieamsuwan; p16: Shutterstock/Nicolas Primola; p17: Shutterstock/Alhovik; p18: Shutterstock/svetok30; p19: Shutterstock/R Carner; p20: Shutterstock/belyaev.photo; p21: Shutterstock/Csanad Kiss; p22: Shutterstock/FashionStock.com; p23: Shutterstock/Sergey Nivens; p24: Shutterstock/Mike Workman; p25: Shutterstock/Fizkes; p26: Shutterstock/Zakirov Aleksey; p27: Shutterstock/Africa Studio; p28: Shutterstock/DedMityay; p29: Shutterstock/Rido.

Printed in the United States of America

Contents

Help! How Do I Write Well?

#Help! Your English teacher has asked you to write a story. And for geography you have to write a **report** about the natural world. It's really freaking you out! Worries about writing well can send any student into a spin. But, fear not—help is at hand! With a few simple tools, writing well is easy. And it can be really fun, too!

Writing—What's So Great?

Before we hop into learning how to write well, let's first think about why great writing is important. Different types of writing help a writer achieve various important things. To begin with, you can express, or show, your **opinion** in writing. This type of writing includes the writer's point of view. It has facts and reasons that back up that viewpoint. To express your opinion, you could write a blog about why you are passionate about a sport, for example. Another type of writing is informational text. This type of text explains ideas and information. You could use it to write instructions. For example, informational text could tell a friend how to care for a pet. A narrative text features real or imagined events and experiences. It has characters and a lot of details and descriptions. You could use a spooky narrative to terrify your friends at Halloween!

You Can Hack It!

Can you think of some situations in which being able to write different types of text could be useful? What are they?

Students: step into the library! It's the perfect place to start any writing project.

Reach Out with Writing

Writing well takes time and patience, but the results are amazing! Just remember—once you have your words on paper, others will read them. That could connect you with a ton of different people.

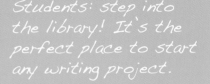

Where Do I Start?

OK, so you've been given a writing assignment. But how do you put it together? Well, all great writers follow some basic steps, like the ones below, to help them shape their writing project. Follow them to help you plan what will fill your page:

- **Research** *and take notes*: First, find information about your topic. Then take notes.
- *Shape it up*: Next, put your notes in order in an **outline**.
- *Write*: Now, follow your outline to write your text.
- *Review and* **revise**: Finally, read your text. Think about how you can improve your writing. Then, revise your text.

Chapter One

Help! How Do I Write Opinion Text?

#SayWhat?! The best opinion writing comes from strong feelings. If you are asked to write an opinion piece, always choose something you care about. For example, write about how much homework should be given! You'll find it easier to get your views across if they are about something that is important to you and that you are interested in.

Who Cares?

How much you care about the topic you are writing about will show in your work:

- Your author "voice" is your individual writing style. It's what makes your writing different from anyone else's. Your writing voice is created by your choice of words. It is also shaped by the tone, or style of writing, of your piece, such as how serious it is. Remember —the more you care about your piece, the stronger your voice will be.

#Hack: Passionate about the **environment**? Then show it in your writing!

- When you care about the subject of your piece, you'll put more effort into writing about it. It will then read well.
- If you care about the topic, you'll enjoy writing the piece more.

Back It Up

Your argument will be much stronger if you can back it up with facts and **evidence**. You can research facts from websites, library books, and encyclopedias. You can also use newspapers and magazines. Your local world can be used for research, too. For example, you could interview local people and friends about your topic.

Write It Down

Always make notes about the facts you find. For example, you could write down key words to remind you of your fact. You could also write a shorter version of the information you find. It is important to remember that for every opinion you give, you should have at least one example or some **factual** proof to support your opinion.

Don't forget to research and write down facts that can help support your argument.

What Should I Trust? #Help!

When researching, choose your **sources** carefully. This is because some are far better than others. For example, most **reference** books are good choices because they have been **edited**, then chosen by a librarian. However, anyone can put up a website. Try to choose websites ending in .edu, .gov, or .org. They will have been created by reliable sources, such as universities or government departments. Not all websites are created equal, so always make sure you use a good source.

How Do I Hook a Reader?

The first part of your opinon writing is super important. After all, it draws your reader in and makes them want to read more. The first paragraph of your written piece is called the introduction, and it's important for all types of writing.

A great introduction captures the reader. It makes them want to read and read!

What's It All About?

A good introduction tells your reader what the piece of writing is about. It usually includes a short **summary**. These are the aims of a good introduction:

- Provide the reader with an outline of what they can expect from your piece.
- Put across your particular viewpoint.
- Get the reader hooked, excited, and wanting to read more and more!

Last Before First?

Some writers like to write the main part of the text and the conclusion, or ending, before they write the introduction. Sounds crazy, right?! Well, there is a reason for this seemingly strange method. The introduction should tell the reader what the piece is about, and that can be a lot easier to do after writing the whole piece. Good authors also write about something that is super interesting to most people right from the start.

Can you remember reading a book that you just couldn't put down? Well, I bet it had a really great introduction and you were hooked from the get-go. Sometimes, it can be difficult to think of something that can really grab your reader's attention. It helps to remember that important issues, such as the future of polar bears, almost always capture a person's **focus**.

Read On, Reader!

Your introduction needs to be exciting to hook your reader. But how do authors add spice to their words? Many authors use one of three ways to fire up an introduction:

- *Add an anecdote*: This is a very short story, often a personal one.
- *Throw in a fact or a quote*: This should be relevant, or connected, to the topic. If it is from an expert on the subject you are writing about, that's really powerful.
- *Ask a rhetorical question*: This is a question to which you don't expect an answer. Try to make sure it grabs the reader's attention. For example, "Are you willing to watch polar bears die of starvation?"

Most people care about polar bears. A topic like that grabs their attention.

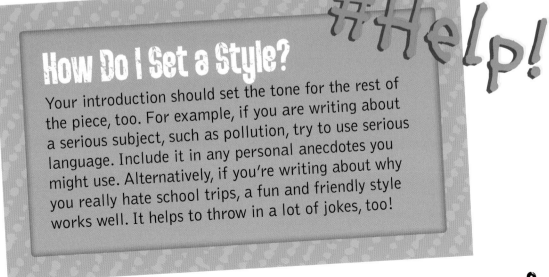

#Help!

How Do I Set a Style?

Your introduction should set the tone for the rest of the piece, too. For example, if you are writing about a serious subject, such as pollution, try to use serious language. Include it in any personal anecdotes you might use. Alternatively, if you're writing about why you really hate school trips, a fun and friendly style works well. It helps to throw in a lot of jokes, too!

How Do I Make a Plan?

OK, so now you have a great introduction. Your reader is hooked, and ready to read more. But what comes next? Well, the next step is to carefully organize your opinion piece. That is because, before you construct the main part of any writing project, you first need to plan it out. A plan is also known as an outline. It will make sure that your writing is interesting and easy to follow. And, most importantly, a plan also makes writing a piece a whole lot easier for the author!

An example of a strong fact is: Scientific evidence shows that eating apples keeps people healthy. Make sure you back up your arguments with similarly strong and powerful evidence.

The Back-Up Plan

If you need to write an opinion piece, you'll probably have several reasons to back up your opinion. Most people start their opinion piece with their weakest argument and end it with their strongest. Plan to cover one idea at a time, like this:

1. What do you think?
2. Why do you think that?
3. How do you know?

By following this plan, first you give your opinion. Then you give the reason for it. Finally, you give examples or facts to back up that reason.

Making Words Work

All great writing flows, or moves easily, from one idea to the next. For example, take a look at this piece of writing: "Cats are the best pets—they are independent.

My cat doesn't need walking, but dogs need a lot of walking." Pretty boring, huh? Now take a look at the same information, but written in an entirely different way: "I absolutely think that cats make the best pets because they are so independent. For example, my cat doesn't need walking at all. On the other hand, dogs need to be walked a lot because they are far more demanding than cats!" Better, right? "**Transition**" words such as "for example, because, on the other hand" make the text flow from one idea to the next, just like links in a chain.

What Words Should I Use?

#Help!

Try out these transition words to make your writing flow:

- *Introduce similar ideas*: additionally, besides, so, too, also, likewise, as well as, another, or finally.
- *Introduce a different idea*: in contrast, on the other hand, yet, despite, still, other people say, but, although, or, however.
- *Continue an idea*: as a result, consequently, so, it follows that, therefore, or eventually.

"I like cats but I also like dogs, despite what other people might say." Can you spot the transition words?

Chapter Two

Help! How Do I Write Information?

#TellMeMore! Informational text is designed to inform, or tell people things. Unlike opinion pieces, informational text gives people information without expressing an opinion about it. You probably read this type of writing every day in your schoolbooks. But how can *you* tell people things by writing really great informational text? Read on, rookie writer!

Coming Up with a Title

The first thing to do when writing informational text is to come up with a title. However, this can sometimes feel challenging, even for the most experienced writers. Don't panic if you feel that you are struggling. Try **brainstorming** ideas for a title by writing down whatever comes into your head. Ask friends and family to pitch in and help. Another useful trick is to use a question in the title of your text. It will catch a reader's interest. For example, "How do elephants care for their young?"

#Hack: Classmates can be a great help if you are struggling to come up with a title for your work.

Writing a book about orcas? Make sure that you cover everything your reader might want to know.

Get to Know Your Audience

Next, research your information. To do this, you need to know who your audience is. Ask yourself questions like these: Who is the text aimed at? How old are they? What do they need to know to understand and learn from your piece of informational text? Then, make notes as you research.

Sort It Out!

Always remember that informational text should provide clear information about a subject. When you begin to write, carefully consider and pinpoint the main ideas you want to cover in your text. To help figure out what these main ideas are, ask yourself what the important things are that you want your audience to learn. Once you have the answers, you can organize your research into groups. For example, when writing a book about orcas, make notes about where orcas swim, what they eat, and how they communicate, or talk to each other.

#Help!

How Can I Be Interesting?

When you're researching, look out for interesting details that will make your writing exciting. They will make your writing far more interesting to read. Tell your readers something new that they probably don't yet know. For example, if you're writing about light, include the interesting detail that there is no such thing as moonlight because the moon reflects, or bounces back, the sun's light.

How Do I Get Organized?

Organizing your writing is really important. That is because your readers will get much more from your informational text if it is arranged well and easy to follow. Imagine your writing is like a storeroom. Everything needs to be in its right place so you can find it easily. Labeling will make your writing world a whole lot easier to work in.

Add a Heading, Pen a Paragraph

Headings perform the same important role as labels: They tell the reader what's in the text below it. Headings are usually short—around one to five words long. They help the reader navigate, or find their way around, the book. Under each heading, you might have one or more paragraphs. A paragraph is usually made up of several sentences about a single idea.

You can't find what you need in a messy bedroom—and you can't find what you need in messy writing!

How Do I Build a List?

If you want to include several short pieces of information, you can put them in a bulleted list. Here is an example of a bulleted list:

• Bulleted points can be short and snappy.
• Some bulleted points are complete sentences like this.

Tips for Writing

You have organized your headings and planned what ideas to put into your paragraphs. Now, it's time to start considering how to write the text. Here are some helpful points to guide how you approach the writing stage of your informational text:

• Informational text is usually written in the present **tense**, such as "This is how it works."
• It is normally written in the third person, such as "Tigers are a type of cat."
• It can sometimes be written in the past tense, if it is a historical report. For example, "World War II began in 1939."

Cool Comparisons

You can keep your reader interested by comparing and contrasting things. If you compare two things, you can explain how alike they are. If you contrast two things, you can explain how they are different. For example, "Lions and tigers both have very sharp teeth" or "A lion's roar is much louder than a tiger's."

#Hack: Friends or classmates can lend a helping hand when it comes to organizing your information.

How Do I Use Words and Pictures?

Images help us make sense of information, and they make writing a lot more fun to read! Many informational books are packed with pictures, diagrams, charts, and maps. That is because they help readers to better understand the information in the words. So, what is the best way to add images to your informational writing?

Better Than Words

Illustrations and diagrams are not only interesting, they also express some types of information better than words alone. For example, you might choose to include a cutaway drawing of a volcano in an informational piece about volcanic eruptions.

This cutaway drawing explains the features of a volcano far better than words would.

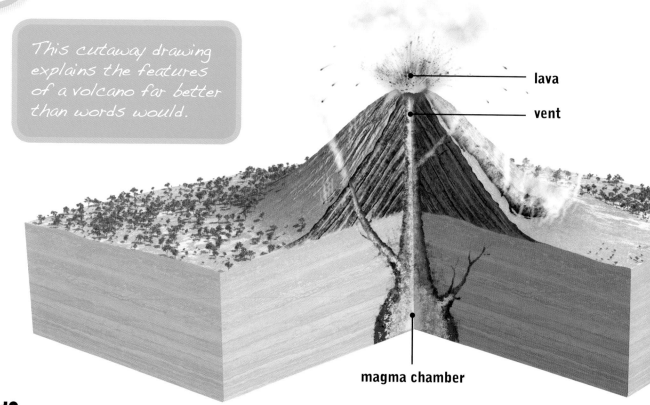

lava

vent

magma chamber

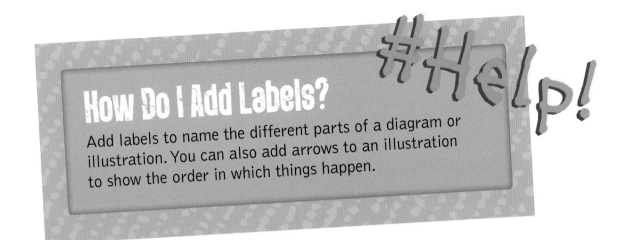

How Do I Add Labels?

Add labels to name the different parts of a diagram or illustration. You can also add arrows to an illustration to show the order in which things happen.

#Help!

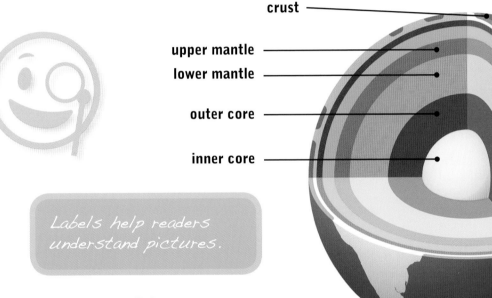

crust
upper mantle
lower mantle
outer core
inner core

Labels help readers understand pictures.

Choosing Pictures

So you know you want to add some images to your informational text. But how do you choose the right ones? Here are some ideas:

- A table or chart is useful for comparing things, such as different animals or rocks.
- A timeline is a bar with dates that show different events. It is useful in a historical report or **biography**.
- Line and bar graphs can show changes over time or compare things. An example is the populations, or numbers of people, of different countries.
- A pie chart quickly shows the different proportions, or amounts, of something, such as different food groups.
- Maps can show different things, such as where important events took place or where bananas are grown and sold.

How Do I Choose My Words?

It is very important to choose words carefully when you are writing informational text. Information must be explained with the correct words, otherwise it can be **misleading**. If you are writing informational text, always try to choose your **vocabulary** carefully and always check your facts.

Words—They're Tricky!

Have you ever wondered why most informational books have some words highlighted with a bold text in the main part of the book, then explained in a glossary at the end? This is because informational texts often use difficult words to explain things. For example, in a text about volcanoes, you might use scientific words such as "lava." In a text about wind power, you might use technical words such as "turbines." These may be difficult words for the reader to understand. However, the topic cannot be explained without them, so don't be afraid to use them. The key is to be sure that you understand any words you use and can explain them.

Difficult words such as "turbine" can be explained to help your reader understand the information.

Check It Out!

You also need to read through your text after writing it. This is to make sure it reads well and is free of mistakes. It is a process called editing. To edit all types of written work, you must read through it carefully and check for the following:

- Are all the words spelled correctly?
- Are the **grammar** and punctuation correct, such as having periods and commas in the right places?
- Do the headings **relate** to what is in the text below them?
- Do you cover one idea in each new paragraph?
- Do all the paragraphs relate to the topic?
- Does everything make sense?

Should I Use a Printout?

Even if you have already started using a computer to type up your work, it might be easier to print out a copy to edit. You can then use red pen to mark any errors or areas you want to change. You can later make the changes on a computer.

#Help!

You Can Hack It!

Editors always carefully edit the manuscripts, or unedited texts, of books before they are published. What might happen if they did not carry out this important work?

19

Chapter Three
Help! How Do I Write a Story?

#Can'tPutItDown! Stories are amazing reads, aren't they? Do you prefer detective stories or romances? Do you like comics best? Or do you love them all equally? There are many types of narratives available. So, when writing a narrative, your first job is to choose which type!

So Many Stories

Narrative is a more technical word for story. It means an account of connected events. A narrative can be a **fictional** or true story. It can also be a combination of imaginary and factual events. Imaginary tales include mystery, romance, and adventure. They also include comic strips, **myths**, fairy tales, **legends**, and **fables**. A factual or nonfiction narrative might describe a historical event or a recent event from the news. A biography is a written account of another person's life, such as a famous politician or musician. An autobiography is a written account of a person's life, but one that is written by that person.

A narrative can be a true story of survival in the wild.

Buzzing? Start Planning!

Once you are buzzing with amazing ideas for your story, it's best to plan it through before you start to write it up. Here are some things to think about:

- *Plot*: What is going to happen and what is the main thread of the story?
- *Setting*: Where will the story take place? What time period is it set in —the past, present, or future?
- *Characters*: Who will the main characters in your story be? It is helpful to make a mindmap or a chart showing some of the ideas for your narrative.

> Think carefully about your characters. Remember, the **hero** of a tale doesn't have to be human!

#Help!

How Do I Start My Story?

A good introduction is important for an informational or opinion piece. Some strong opening lines are vital for a narrative, too. Look at a few of your favorite books to see how they begin. What do other authors do to get their readers' attention right from the beginning?

Who Will Tell My Story?

The voice that tells your story has an important role to play. After all, it shapes how readers hear your story and **interpret** the words within it. So how do you choose this narrator, or storyteller? There are three types of narrators and they each tell the story in a different way:

- *The Narrator Who Knows All*: This is not a character in the story, but a person who knows what is going on and is in all the characters' minds. For example, "Sam is playing soccer in the playground, thinking about his dinner. Jess is in class, daydreaming about her party."
- *A Third-Person Narrator*: This is when the author tells the story from one character's **perspective**. For example, "Sam thinks about what to have for dinner as he kicks the ball. He wonders what Jess is doing."
- *First-Person Narrator*: This is when the narrator is a character in the story—a person who speaks for and about themselves. For example, in Sam's voice it would read, "I think I'll have pizza for dinner. I wonder where Jess is now."

#Hack: You can base a narrator or a character on someone famous.

Why Should I Build a File?

A file of facts gives information about your characters, such as how old they are and who their friends are. It might also tell who is in their family, and what their activities are. Even if you don't actually use the facts, it will help you imagine that the characters are real.

Bring Them to Life!

You've decided on the narrator, but what about the other characters? How can you make them real? There are several ways:

- Decide on the appearance of your characters. That will help give them an identity. For example, are they tall or short, blue- or brown-eyed? Do they have long or curly hair? What clothes do they wear? You could look at pictures in magazines for ideas.
- Base the character on someone you know. This could be a friend, a family member, or even a celebrity. This will help you describe how they look and react to things.
- Make them more human. Give good characters bad and unlikable habits or weaknesses, and give bad characters moments of likability and goodness, too.

You Can Hack It!

Why do you think it is important to paint a visual picture of a character for your reader? How might this help them engage with the story?

How Do I Write Conversations?

When the characters in your story start to speak and move, they really come to life. Description and dialogue, or words spoken between characters, will hook your reader.

How would you describe this scene in your story?

Where It All Happens

The settings of a text are where the scenes in your story take place. Describing the setting of a story adds atmosphere and sparks the reader's imagination. For example, does your story happen on a faraway island? Perhaps it takes place in a busy city of the future, or in a fairy tale castle set in the past? When you've chosen a setting, write a short description of how it might look, sound, feel, and smell to help you write your story.

#Help!

How Do I Build a Word Bank?

Use a **thesaurus** to come up with a "word bank" of awesome **adjectives** that you can use to describe your setting. For example, if your story takes place in a haunted house, you might have a bank of words such as **menacing**, terrifying, spooky, and dangerous.

Show Through Speech

Dialogue reveals things about characters through their speech and their reactions to what other characters say. It also tells the reader important parts of the plot and helps bring scenes to life. Another huge advantage of including dialogue is that it breaks up the text a little, too. That is because a new paragraph begins every time a new character speaks.

Dos and Don'ts

- Never use dialogue instead of a description of an exciting event. For example, rather than a character saying, "Look—an avalanche!" describe the avalanche with exciting adjectives.
- Don't try to cover a conversation with long hellos, goodbyes, or mind-numbing discussions about the weather! Try to skip quickly to the interesting parts—and keep your reader focused.

Find a Fit

Make your dialogue credible, or believable. You can do this by using styles of speaking that fit the characters. For example, most grandmothers wouldn't say "That's really cool!" Instead, they'd say, "That's lovely!"

Try to make dialogue between characters, such as a mom and daughter, believable.

How Do I Keep Readers Reading?

Have you read a story that had you gripped with every word? Were you hooked from start to finish? Great narratives build up a feeling of **suspense**, excitement, or **intrigue**. That keeps the reader reading and eager to turn every single page. They have strong beginnings, middles, and endings, which is sometimes described as the "narrative arc."

A Story's Journey

An arc is like a hill: It goes up, then it goes down again. This is how the action works in most narratives, too:

- In the beginning, the characters, setting, and time of the story are set out. Events then start to happen that build up to the middle of the story.
- In the middle of the story, the main character faces some type of problem or complication. There, they have their main adventures.
- At the end of the story, any problems that took place within it are solved. Complications are fixed.

Make your characters face exciting challenges.

*#Hack: Working with other writers is fun, so **collaborate** and check each other's stories.*

Link It Up

Don't forget to use a variety of transition words and phrases to link the stages in your narrative. They will help readers know when there is a shift from one time or setting to another.

Check It Over

When you have written a first draft (a first attempt at your narrative), read it through carefully. Then, edit it. Check the spelling, punctuation, and grammar. This is also your chance to make sure the story makes sense and flows well. For example, if the main character solves their problem using a particular skill, it might be good to show them using that skill early in the story. If one character seems a little unbelievable, you could add some dialogue or description to bring them to life.

How Do I Check the Flow? #Help!

One of the best ways to check that your story or narrative is flowing well is to read it out loud to yourself. You'll be surprised! It can be so much easier to spot errors or places where part of a story is weak or missing when you read it out loud. You could also have somebody else read your story to you.

Conclusion
Help! How Do I Finish?

#Phew! You have nearly finished, but here comes another important part—the ending! It is the last thing your reader will read, and you really want to make it great. But, how do you put together an epic ending?

Twists in the Tale

At the end of a narrative, try to end your story on a "high." You will also need to wrap up the characters' problems and the events of the story. Some writers talk about what a character learned from their experiences. They may end with a "twist"—a surprise that the readers could never have foreseen! Perhaps you could write a **cliffhanger**." It keeps your reader guessing about what happens next to the characters in your story. You could always add that, to find out, they must read your next tale!

You Can Hack It!

What do you think are the advantages of ending your story on a cliffhanger with lots of unsolved mysteries? Give reasons for your answers.

How Do I Talk to My Reader?

In an opinion piece, you might like to end your conclusion by talking directly to your readers. You could ask them a question to see if you have persuaded them to agree with your opinion. You might also encourage them to take action. For example, if you have been writing about pollution due to burning oil, you could suggest the readers try car-sharing or walking to school.

Back to the Beginning

Before writing your conclusion, reread the whole text. Refresh your memory about what has happened in the story. Often, a good conclusion brings the reader full circle by tying together the beginning and the ending. For example, a character might refer to a warning given at the start of a story.

Nothing New

In an informational text or opinion piece, the conclusion or last paragraph should not introduce any new information. The aim is to link your conclusion to the rest of your report and sum up what you've said before, without simply repeating yourself. Many people refer back to their introduction, then show how they have explained the facts. They might also show how their examples have combined to support their opinion.

Awesome Endings

Remember, your conclusion is probably the main thing that your readers will remember about your text. That is because it is the last thing that they read. So make it awesome!

And finally—don't forget to enjoy writing. Who knows, maybe you could write a future bestseller!

Glossary

adjectives descriptive words. They tell us how something looks, feels, smells, or tastes

biography a person's life story

brainstorming generating a list of ideas and solutions to solve a problem

cliffhanger a chapter, page, or narrative that ends in suspense

collaborate work together

edited checked for mistakes and corrected

environment the natural world

evidence facts and information collected to support things we say

fables short stories that have a moral, or something that shows us the right way to behave

factual related to fact

fictional made up, not real

focus attention

grammar the system and structure of language, such as sentences and paragraphs

hero a person or animal admired for achievements and qualities

interpret to explain the meaning of something

intrigue strangeness or mystery

legends stories about mythical or historical figures or events

menacing threatening

misleading leading people away from the truth, not informing people correctly

myths old, traditional stories, often about gods and heroes

opinion a person's views about something

outline a simple plan for a piece of writing

perspective point of view

reference factual text, often a book with information and images

relate connect to

report a written account

research find out about something

revise change something to improve it

sources books or documents used to provide evidence in research

summary short statement giving the main points about something

suspense feeling of excitement and uncertainty about what is going to happen

tense how verbs express time, such as past, present, and future (for example, is, was, will be)

thesaurus a book that lists words and their synonyms

transition movement from one thing to another

vocabulary range of words used

Find Out More

Books

Dakers, Diane. *Environmental Journalism*. Crabtree Publishing, 2018.

Rees, Lexi. *Creative Writing Skills: Over 70 Fun Activities for Children.* Outset Publishing Ltd., 2019.

Rompella, Natalie. *Secrets of Storytelling: A Creative Writing Workbook for Kids.* Rockridge Press, 2020.

Websites

For great tips and ideas about writing reports visit the Writing Reports section at:
kidshealth.org/kid/homework/index.html?tracking=81347_I #cat20956

Find more great tips about writing at:
www.dailywritingtips.com/writing-tips-for-kids

Learn more about how to write well at :
www.youtube.com/watch?v=KcVixTq06bA

Publisher's note to educators and parents:

All the websites featured above have been carefully reviewed to ensure that they are suitable for students. However, many websites change often, and we cannot guarantee that a site's future contents will continue to meet our high standards of educational value. Please be advised that students should be closely monitored whenever they access the Internet.

Index

About the Authors

Sarah Eason has written a wide variety of information books for children on many topics. Louise Spilsbury is an award-winning author who has written hundreds of wonderful books for children. Both love writing, especially for children!